OWLS

LIVING WILD

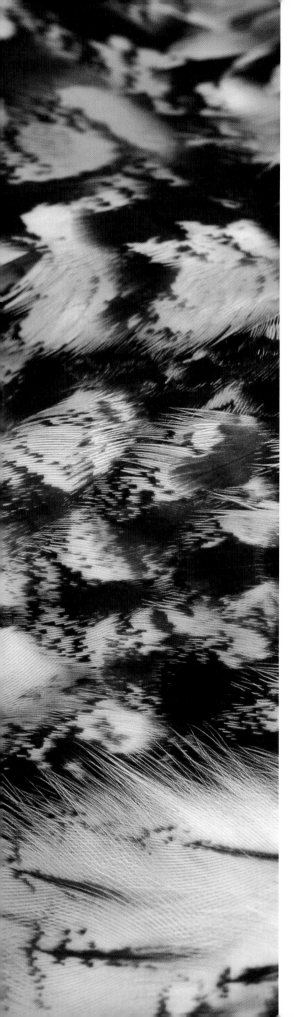

LIVING WILD

Published by Creative Paperbacks
P.O. Box 227, Mankato, Minnesota 56002
Creative Paperbacks is an imprint of The Creative Company
www.thecreativecompany.us

Design and production by Mary Herrmann
Art direction by Rita Marshall
Printed by Corporate Graphics in the United States of America

Photographs by 123RF (Pablo Caridad, Dndavis, Stephen Meese, Paul Ransome, Kuang Ying-Chou), Alamy (Arcticphoto, The Art Archive, Nathan Benn, David Hosking, William Leaman, Peter Arnold, Inc., Photos 12, Picture Press, Paris Pierce, Robert Harding Picture Library Ltd), Corbis (Ron Austing/Frank Lane Picture Agency), Dreamstime (Klomsky, Marilyna, Mirceax, Tom Theodore, Vasiliy Vishneskiy, Bill Warchol), Getty Images (DEA/G. Dagli Orti, Jeff Foott, Art Wolfe, Jeremy Woodhouse), iStockphoto (Ken Canning, Gary Forsyth, Ronald Glovan, Andre Gravel, Cynthia Lindow, Megan Lorenz, Rich Phalin, John Pitcher, Studioworxx, Paul Tessier, Frank Van Den Bergh, Anna Yu)

The Library of Congress has cataloged the hardcover edition as follows:
Gish, Melissa.
Owls / by Melissa Gish.
p. cm. — (Living wild)
Includes bibliographical references and index.
Summary: A look at owls, including their habitats, physical characteristics such as their large and observant eyes, behaviors, relationships with humans, and protected status in the world today.
ISBN 978-1-60818-081-3 (hardcover)
ISBN 978-0-89812-673-0 (pbk)
1. Owls—Juvenile literature. I. Title.

QL696.S8G57 2011
598.9'7—dc22   2010028308

CPSIA: 061313 PO1705

9 8 7 6 5 4 3

OWLS

Melissa Gish

As the sun inches behind a stand of tall ponderosa pines in Washington state's Okanogan

National Forest, a shadowed figure stirs in a thicket.

As the sun inches behind a stand of tall ponderosa pines in Washington state's Okanogan National Forest, a shadowed figure stirs in a thicket. Reddish-brown with white speckles, a male northern saw-whet owl ruffles his feathers, opens his large yellow eyes, and scans the area. "*swEE swEE swEE swEE*," he sings. His repetitive, high-pitched call sounds like a rusty swing. It is the first sound he has made in nearly a year, for these birds sing only during the spring breeding season. In the distance, a female returns the call. The male scans the area, quickly locating a mouse amid the tree branches. Ceasing his call, the male silently swoops down and snatches the unwary mouse in his talons. Then he flaps his wings and rises upward in the darkness. Hoping to mate, the male will carry this prize to the distant female as a gesture of bonding.

WHERE IN THE WORLD THEY LIVE

■ **Eurasian Eagle Owl**
Europe, Asia, northern Africa

■ **Collared Scops Owl**
northern Pakistan to southern China

□ **Common Barn Owl**
worldwide, except polar and desert regions

■ **Great Horned Owl**
the Americas

■ **Northern Pygmy-owl**
forests in western North America

■ **Snowy Owl**
Canada, northern Europe and Asia

■ **Oriental Hawk Owl**
Indonesia, Sri Lanka, Japan

■ **Short-eared Owl**
worldwide, except Australia and Antarctica

The more than 200 owl species are spread around the world, from the Arctic to Australia. Colored squares represent the common locations of eight representative owl species found in the wild today.

SWIFT AND SILENT

T oday, there are more than 10,000 bird species on Earth. About 205 of these are owls, and with few exceptions, they are primarily nocturnal, meaning they are active at night and sleep during the day. Owls are found on every continent except Antarctica and live in every kind of habitat, from dense forests to open prairies. They have **adapted** to a variety of climates, from scorching deserts to frozen tundras. Some species are fighting against the threat of **extinction**, while other populations remain numerous.

The owl, like all birds, is warm-blooded. This means it is able to keep its body temperature at a constant level, no matter what the temperature is outside. Birds may adjust their body temperatures by shivering to warm up and panting to cool down. Birds are covered with feathers; they walk on two legs and lay eggs to reproduce. Owls are classified in the order Strigiformes, a group of raptors, or birds that hunt and eat living things. Eagles, hawks, and falcons are also raptors.

The word "owl" is derived from the sound that owls make. In Latin, *ululare* means "to howl," which is what

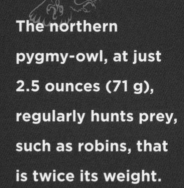

The northern pygmy-owl, at just 2.5 ounces (71 g), regularly hunts prey, such as robins, that is twice its weight.

The elf owl is sometimes known as the Texas elf owl or the dwarf owl, and in Mexico it is called enano.

people believed owls did. Therefore, the word *ulula* was used to describe owls. This word then spread in various forms across Europe. By about A.D. 600, Germans were calling owls *uwila,* and the English used the word *ule.* Four hundred years later, the word had become *owle,* and in another four centuries it was shortened to the word we use today.

The oldest known owl fossils are more than 50 million years old. *Ornimegalonyx,* an owl species that existed about 30,000 years ago, was twice as big as today's largest owl. It fed on giant rodents the size of German shepherds. Over millions of years, owls **evolved** into two families: barn owls and typical owls. The 21 species of barn owl share a characteristic heart-shaped face, but the typical owls differ greatly in appearance, **plumage,** behavior, and size. For example, the world's largest owl, the Eurasian eagle owl, is 28 inches long (70 cm), while the smallest, the elf owl, is less than 5.5 inches (14 cm) long. Owl vocalizations vary as well, from the steady, clarinet-like call of the flammulated owl to the sporadic trilling of the scops owl.

All owls are beneficial to their environments. They eat rodents and insects that might otherwise cause damage

Female Eurasian eagle owls weigh four to nine pounds (1.8–4 kg), while males weigh about three to seven pounds (1.4–3.2 kg).

Eastern screech owls are often mistaken for young great horned owls because of their small ear tufts.

to crops or lead to human illness. Some of the largest owls, such as the great horned and great gray owls of North America, are typically the primary predators of small prey in their forest habitats. However, smaller owls such as Eastern screech owls must compete with larger owls and other birds of prey for food. And despite their **camouflage**, ground-dwelling burrowing owls often fall prey themselves to goshawks, eagles, and larger owls.

While many owls around the world, including the boreal owl of North America and Europe (where it is called Tengmalm's owl), enjoy stable populations, some species, such as northeast Asia's Blakiston's fish owl, are now endangered. Such endangerment is often caused by human **encroachment**. Fewer than 20 owl species live in North America, and the populations of some, including the common barn owl, which has been affected by chemical use in agriculture, have fallen sharply in recent years.

Certain aspects of the owl's body have helped it to remain a successful hunter since its earliest days on Earth. The owl's large, round head features forward-facing eyes that may account for up to 20 percent of the face. Each eye captures light independently, which means one pupil may become larger than the other if a shadow falls across one side of the owl's face. The eyes are stationary, so they do not rotate in their sockets like human eyes do. To compensate for this, owls can twist their necks around so far that they can see behind themselves.

Like a pair of **satellite** dishes, the two sections of the face around the eyes—each called a facial disc—function to collect and amplify sounds that are then directed toward the ears, which are set at slightly different heights on the owl's head. Owls have elongated ear openings— spanning nearly the length of the entire head in some

Great horned owls are sometimes called tiger owls because their underside markings resemble stripes.

Great horned owls have exceptionally strong feet and talons, allowing them to carry prey as large as a goose.

When alarmed, owls may raise their ear tufts high to make themselves look as large as possible.

species—that are covered by a single or double membrane called an operculum. This flap of skin can be extended or contracted by special muscles around the ears, allowing the owl to capture sounds from all directions.

Because the ears are set at different heights in some owls, one of the owl's ears will pick up a sound a split second before the other ear. The owl then swivels its head until the sound reaches both ears at the same time, which tells the owl exactly where the source of the sound is located—up or down, in front or behind. Once they locate prey, owls launch surprise attacks from above. Most owl species are able to do this because of a unique feature that renders them silent in flight.

When other birds fly, air passes over the surface of the wing, creating a rippling of air behind the wing—and a whooshing sound. Most owls have a stiff row of fringe, called fimbriae, on the edge of each primary wing feather. As air passes over these comblike feathers, the rippling effect is minimized, muffling its sound. All nocturnal owls have fimbriae, but the few diurnal species—those that hunt during the day, such as the northern pygmy-owl and snowy owl—do not.

Owls capture prey with their sharp talons, two of which are located on the front toes and two on the back toes. These talons are made of keratin, the same material found in human fingernails. Owls do not chew their food. They use their hooked beaks to tear their prey into chunks or swallow it whole. About 20 hours after the nutritious part of a meal is digested, the indigestible portion—consisting of bones and fur or feathers—is **regurgitated** in the form of a single, hard mass called a pellet. Owl pellets play an important role in the owl's environment, providing shelter and food for tiny organisms such as insect larvae, beetles, moths, and fungi.

Male snowy owls may nest with multiple females and hunt for food to feed more than one set of offspring.

Great gray owls use nests that have been abandoned by other birds during their springtime mating season.

NIGHTTIME HUNTERS

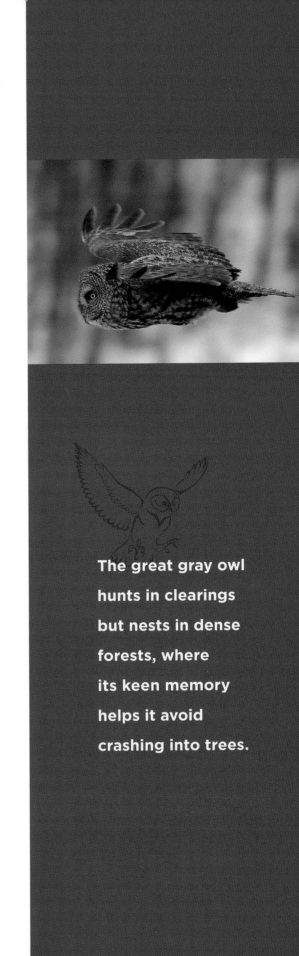

Most species of owl can live up to 20 years. Males and females mature at the same time. Some species reach maturity and are ready to mate at age two, while others do not mate until they are five years old. Most owls remain with a single mate throughout one breeding season, and they may rejoin each other year after year. Some stay together for a full year to raise their young and then separate to find different mates. A few species, including the tawny owl, remain with a single mate for life, but if one dies, the other will find a new partner.

Most owls live in established territories apart from each other. Some species **migrate** seasonally, spending winters in warmer climates and returning home to mate, usually in early spring. Courtship begins when a male calls and a female answers. Once a male and female are near each other, the male may begin a series of impressive aerial acrobatics called flight displays. Strong flight skills are an indication of an owl's ability to be a good provider.

One type of display is the wing-clapping flight. The male flies high into the air—up to 1,500 feet (457 m)—in

The great gray owl hunts in clearings but nests in dense forests, where its keen memory helps it avoid crashing into trees.

a spiral, striking his wing tips together under his body. Then he takes a dive before swooping up suddenly, ending with a wing clap. He repeats this action several times. Finally, he dives sharply downward and lands near the female. A female watching this display may call out her approval to the male.

While flight displays serve to impress future mates, the behavior that establishes trust between two owls is courtship feeding. A male takes prey to a female, dropping it near her as a gesture of affection. For some species, such as barn owls, such feeding is necessary for reproduction. Being fed by males allows females to gain weight and obtain the energy required for egg laying.

In general, owls do not build nests. Tree-nesting owls, such as great horned owls, take over nests abandoned by hawks or ravens. Cavity-nesting owls, such as barred owls, may nest in the holes of buildings or in man-made nest boxes, and various eagle-owl species nest in the crevices of rock ledges. Ground-nesting owls may scratch or burrow to create a nest area. The snowy owl nests in hollows in the ground, which it lines with plant matter. Burrowing owls prefer to use underground burrows

The ferruginous pygmy-owl, found in Arizona and places south, often nests in cactus cavities made by woodpeckers.

Owlets, like other baby birds, do not need water, as they get moisture from the food their parents feed them.

abandoned by small animals such as gophers, but if the ground is very soft, they may dig their own holes. Some owls, including short-eared owls, simply nest in tall grass.

In 9 out of 10 bird species, males are larger than females, but in owls, this characteristic is reversed. Some scientists speculate that this is related to reproduction. Larger females can produce more eggs and can create more heat energy to **incubate** those eggs. Also, while male owls are out hunting for food, female owls remain in the nest and defend their offspring from predators such as larger owls or other raptors; therefore, they must be larger and stronger. Depending on the species, female owls can be up to 40 percent heavier than males, but females may then lose around 30 percent of their body weight after they have incubated their eggs.

Most female owls lay between two and six eggs at a usual rate of one egg every other day. Some cold-climate species, such as the snowy owl, may lay up to 12 eggs to ensure the survival of at least some. In years when prey is sparse, owls lay fewer eggs because there will not be enough food to feed a large family. All owl species lay white eggs. A group of eggs is called a clutch. Like all birds' eggs, owl eggs must be incubated while the baby owls, called owlets, are developing inside. Female owls incubate their eggs for 22 to 35 days. The first egg laid is the first to hatch, which means the eldest hatchling could be as much as two weeks older than its youngest sibling.

Using its **egg tooth**, the hatchling chips through the hard shell of its egg. This may take between 12 and 48 hours. Newly hatched owlets have soft **down** stuck to their moist bodies, but within an hour they are dry, and the down becomes fluffy. Owlets are immediately able to eat meat that their mother brings them. The owlets are fed anything from grasshoppers and earthworms to mice,

Long-eared owls use nests made by such birds as crows or magpies and lay three to eight eggs at a time.

gophers, and snakes. Devouring more than its own body weight in food each day, an owlet grows quickly, and some species, such as the great horned owl, gain as much as one ounce (28 g) per day during the first month of life.

By the time an owlet is about three weeks old, feathers begin to replace its down. Soon it can flap its wings and bounce around the nest floor. As it gains strength, an owlet may leave the nest to explore its surroundings and stretch its wings, but it will never wander far, still depending on its mother for food and protection from predators. Young owls may stay with their mothers for up to five months.

Owls groom and clean their feathers, a practice called preening, but, like most birds, they cannot clean their own faces. Because bird feathers suffer from everyday wear and tear, owls and other birds go through a period called molting during which their feathers fall out and are replaced by new ones. The feathers do not fall out all at once, so grown owls are always able to fly.

When an owl is ready to leave the nest and establish its own territory, it usually chooses an area within 10 miles (16 km) of its home, but some species may travel as far as

150 miles (241 km) to find an unoccupied territory with suitable prey. Most adult owls have no natural enemies other than larger raptors. Humans have the biggest effect on owl populations around the world. Destroying owl habitat and shooting, trapping, and poisoning owls are practices that have reduced the numbers of many owl species—including Peru's long-whiskered owlet (so named for its small size), which was discovered in 1976—to the brink of extinction.

Between losing down and gaining adult plumage, young owls develop feathers and coloring more similar to adults'.

The owl carved on the coffin of an Egyptian priest, dating back to the 4th century B.C., is most likely a barn owl.

BIRDS OF MYSTERY

T hroughout history, owls have enjoyed significant status in the spiritual and artistic traditions of many world **cultures**. Some cultures revered owls; others feared them. Many artifacts from those cultures survive and show owls being used to symbolize knowledge, wisdom, fertility, fear, and death. Around 10,000 B.C., early humans living in the Victoria River region of north-central Australia painted rock art at a place known as Jigaigarn. The image of Gordol the Owl is an example of one of the earliest-known human drawings. Australian **Aborigines** believed that Gordol was a supernatural being who helped create balance in the world. To this day, a large boulder stands balanced on a tiny base at the site of the owl rock art to symbolize Gordol's steadying presence.

Such petroglyphs have been discovered elsewhere around the world. In France, a roughly 30,000-year-old owl petroglyph was found in the Chauvet Cave, and in Guatemala, a country in Central America, artifacts have been discovered that show how the ancient Maya used the owl as a symbol of power and resurrection. The Maya

An owl ornament made by the Moche people of Peru around A.D. 300 is covered with locally mined gold.

The ancient Egyptian writing system called hieroglyphics used the symbol of the owl to represent the "m" sound.

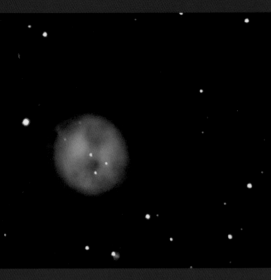

Scientists believe that the Owl Nebula, discovered in 1781, formed about 6,000 years ago.

The ancient Romans believed that dreaming about an owl was unlucky and would cause one to be robbed or shipwrecked.

called the screech owl *Mo An*, meaning "bird of death," and the Mayan death god, *Ah Puch*, was believed to have the body of a man and the head of an owl. People of Mayan descent still fear *Ah Puch*, whom they call *Yum Cimil*, meaning "lord of death."

An owl's eyes are its most striking feature, and they are depicted on masks found in Alaska. The Yupik people used the short-eared owl as the model for ceremonial masks worn during dances that connected the people spiritually to their gods. The owl's large eyes represent its ability to see into the darkness of the unknown. Looking back at humans from the darkness of outer space is the Owl **Nebula**, located 2,600 light years from Earth and part of the constellation Ursa Major. The nebula was named for the two dark spots that resemble an owl's facial discs.

In Chinese culture, the owl's eyes and its ability to rotate its head have earned the owl a reputation as an all-seeing clairvoyant, or one who can tell the future. Such magical images of owls also occur in the islands of the Bahamas, located in the Atlantic Ocean south of the United States, where legends tell of mischievous, elf-like creatures called chickcharnies. These little people have

owlish characteristics, complete with tails, red eyes, and the ability to turn their heads around. It is believed that seeing a chickcharnie will bring a person lifelong good luck.

Because of their association with darkness and the night sky, owls are considered in many cultures to be spiritual messengers between the gods and humans. In ancient Greek **mythology**, Athena, the goddess of wisdom, was represented by the owl. Being visited by an owl was considered a good thing in Greece, but this was not the case everywhere. To this day, many African cultures call owls witch birds and consider them to be evil spirits. In West Africa, an owl perched outside a window

Historically, the Greek goddess Athena was known for her gray, shining eyes, and an owl always accompanied her.

Owls in Chinese artwork are depicted as being mischievous, owing to a traditional belief that young owls devour their parents.

is considered to be a bad omen or even a messenger of death. However, in Asian nations such as Japan, owls are welcome guardians against sickness and starvation; in India, owls are said to bring good fortune, as the owl is the symbol of the Hindu goddess of wealth, Lakshmi.

Many **indigenous** peoples of the North American plains believed the owl had special powers that no other animals possessed, and these powers varied among the species of owl. The Oglala Sioux wore snowy owl feathers as a symbol of bravery and because they believed that wearing such feathers could increase a person's vision. The Cheyenne believed the body of the short-eared owl possessed healing properties, and they wore other owl feathers on their shields to help them see in the dark and travel silently. Because the owl is a stealthy hunter, many tribes called on the owl's power to aid them in hunting. The Hidatsa held a ceremony before hunting in which the head, two wings, and two claws of a speckled owl were used to call bison to the hunting grounds.

Owls' associations with wisdom and magic have persisted through the ages. From British author T. H. White's tales of King Arthur and his Knights of the

Under U.S. and Canadian law, only certain American Indians or First Nations people are allowed to possess owl feathers.

Round Table came Archimedes, the feathered companion of Merlin the magician. Walt Disney Pictures based the film *The Sword in the Stone* (1963) on young Arthur's adventures in White's epic *The Once and Future King* (1958). Other Disney films featuring owls include *Bambi* (1942), in which the wise teacher of the woods is Owl, and *Sleeping Beauty* (1959), in which Owl is one of Princess Aurora's friends. One of the most famous owls in modern literature and film is Hedwig, the messenger owl in J. K. Rowling's Harry Potter series. In the films, Hedwig's character was played by several different snowy owls.

Kathryn Lasky's Guardians of Ga'Hoole is a 15-book fantasy series featuring Soren, a young barn owl, who joins a resistance movement against forces of evil in his world. *Legend of the Guardians: The Owls of Ga'Hoole* (2010) is a three-dimensional animated movie based on the first three books in the series. On television, the long-running (1968–2001) educational children's show *Mister Rogers' Neighborhood* featured puppets in the Neighborhood of Make-Believe, including X the Owl. On the show, this tree-dwelling character shared with viewers his assignments from the Owl Correspondence School.

Owls also represent sports teams from all around the world, from England's Sheffield Wednesday Football Club, called the Owls, to Temple University in Philadelphia, Pennsylvania, the first school in the U.S. to adopt the owl as its official mascot. The sports teams at Rice University in Houston, Texas, are also the Owls, and they are cheered on by their mascot, Sammy the Owl. Apart from sports, other institutions, such as ISAE in Paris, also choose owls as mascots. This top European school for aerospace engineering is represented by the little owl, a symbol of wisdom that has historically been tied to the goddess Athena.

The Archimedes character in The Sword in the Stone *is sometimes cranky but often helpful to Merlin and young Arthur.*

THE OWL

When cats run home and light is come,
And dew is cold upon the ground,
And the far-off stream is dumb,
And the whirring sail goes round,
And the whirring sail goes round;
Alone and warming his five wits,
The white owl in the belfry sits.

When merry milkmaids click the latch,
And rarely smells the new-mown hay,
And the cock hath sung beneath the thatch
Twice or thrice his roundelay,
Twice or thrice his roundelay;
Alone and warming his five wits,
The white owl in the belfry sits.

by Alfred, Lord Tennyson (1809–92)

SILENTLY SLIPPING AWAY

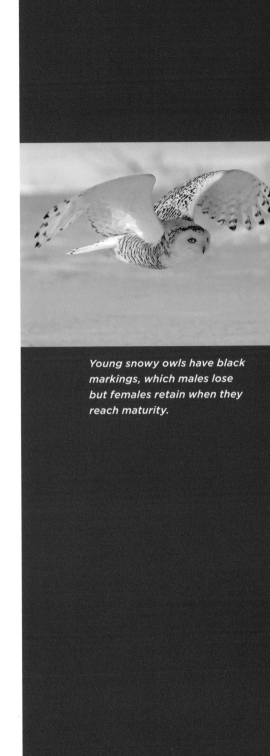

Young snowy owls have black markings, which males lose but females retain when they reach maturity.

O wls are underresearched and poorly understood for the most part, which makes them difficult to protect as cities expand and forestland is converted to farmland. They are often elusive birds as well, making their capture for data collection exceedingly difficult. Some owl species, such as the common barn owl and the burrowing owl, are abundant, but others are endangered. While research and breeding programs keep captive owls all over the world, scientists and conservationists know that protecting owls in their own habitats is vital to owls' long-term survival.

Most research projects involving owls are conducted by small organizations or even individuals interested in owl conservation. Norman Smith of the Blue Hills Trailside Museum in Milton, Massachusetts, is one such individual. Smith has been studying snowy owls since 1981. Snowy owls are vital to the Arctic **food chain** because they mostly eat small rodents called lemmings, which feed on vegetation. Too many lemmings can lead to devastating losses of Arctic mosses and plants, which feed other animals such as caribou.

Smith's research involves capturing and banding owls, sometimes attaching **Global Positioning System** (GPS) tracking devices to them. The devices weigh less than two ounces (56.7 g) and run on a battery that lasts one to three years. They are attached to the owl by a harness that fits over the bird's wings like a backpack, with a strap stretching across the stomach. This harness is designed to fall off when the battery dies. The device sends an electronic signal that is picked up by a weather satellite. The data that is gathered helps researchers follow the migratory patterns of the snowy owls—vital information to the conservation of these important birds.

The Owl Research Institute, located in the Ninepipes Center for Wildlife Research and Education in western Montana, has been conducting field research on a variety of owl species for nearly 30 years. Their studies of snowy owls began in Barrow, Alaska, in 1992. Confirming Smith's research, the Owl Research Institute found that its population of snowy owls was highly migratory as well, moving from Alaska to Canada to Russia. Because these owls cross international boundaries, large-scale international efforts are required to protect their habitats.

In 1987, the snowy owl, which is the only all-white owl, was selected to be the official bird of Quebec.

Fifteen subspecies of Ural owl inhabit woodlands of Europe and Asia and make use of nest boxes.

Habitat destruction caused by human interference is the greatest cause of decline in owl populations. Since most owl species nest in trees, **deforestation** can be devastating. Even the overharvesting of dead trees for firewood can impact owls, as many owls nest in the cavities of dead trees. Many types of owls will make use of artificial nest boxes, but these are not ideal substitutes for abundant trees among which to select territories and nesting sites. While many people place nest boxes high in trees around their homes in efforts to attract owls as natural rodent control, large-scale placement of nest boxes is typically done by organizations to conduct research.

Nest boxes containing cameras are often used to gather data on owl behavior while the owls are nesting and raising their young. Such nest boxes have been used by the Caesar Kleberg Wildlife Research Institute at Texas A&M University to study ferruginous pygmy-owls, by the University of North Carolina in Charlotte to study barred owls, and by California's Sierra Nevada Avian Center to study flammulated owls in New Mexico. The cameras inside the nest boxes are so small that owls do not even seem to notice them. Most cameras have infrared

Nest boxes are often constructed with mirrors to allow the interior of the box to be viewed by researchers.

The juvenile mortality rate of small species such as the spotted owl is 60 to 70 percent, since many larger birds are predators.

capabilities that allow images to be recorded in the dark.

Major owl conservation programs are virtually nonexistent. One of the only large-scale efforts to save an owl species from extinction began in 1989, when the U.S. government established the Interagency Scientific Committee and put it to work creating a conservation program for the northern spotted owl, whose habitat in Oregon, Washington, and California was being destroyed. The study, which led to conflict between environmental groups and the logging industry, helped bring logging in national forests to an end in 1991. The northern spotted owl has since been making a slow recovery but remains on the Endangered Species List because the larger and more aggressive barred owl moved into the protected forests, preying upon spotted owls and forcing them out of their nests.

Among the many smaller programs that help owls is a joint effort between New York state and Canada called the Migration Research Foundation (MRF). Included in its many projects is a close study of the short-eared owl, one of the fastest-declining bird species in North America. Part of the owl's problem, the MRF discovered, is a scarce food supply because their primary prey, voles,

have been declining in numbers due to agriculural use of pesticides, which kill the insects on which voles feed. The owls' lack of food results in their failing to breed.

In Europe, the World Owl Trust, headquartered in the small town of Ravenglass, England, supports the study of all owl species, working to promote habitat management and restoration by conducting research and instituting captive breeding programs in an effort to save threatened and endangered owl species around the world. The organization also maintains a hospital and rehabilitation center for sick and injured owls and other wildlife.

Some species of owl are seriously endangered and require stronger conservation efforts than are typically

Quickly growing too large to share a nest, northern hawk owls move out at three weeks old— before they can even fly.

Blakiston's fish owls hunt by dropping down from low perches directly onto prey in shallow water.

provided for owls. The Blakiston's fish owl, which weighs up to 10 pounds (4.5 kg), is one such endangered owl. It lives along rivers in parts of Russia, China, Korea, and Japan. Because its primary food source is fish, the owl is vulnerable to urban development and dam construction. While populations of this bird in mainland Asia (China and Russia) may stand at several thousand, scientists estimate that fewer than 20 breeding pairs exist in Japan. An ongoing collaborative research project begun in the mid-1990s by the Amur-Ussuri Center for Avian Diversity in Russia, the Russian Academy of Sciences Institute of Biology and Soils, and the University of Minnesota has been working to promote Blakiston's fish owl conservation within Russia's logging industry.

While efforts to conserve owls around the world continue, they are typically small in scope. A number of owl species are in danger of silently slipping away—falling victim to habitat loss, depletion of food sources, and human interference. Such threats can push owls to the brink of extinction—or over. Especially as key rodent predators, owls are invaluable to the web of life and deserve every effort to protect and conserve them.

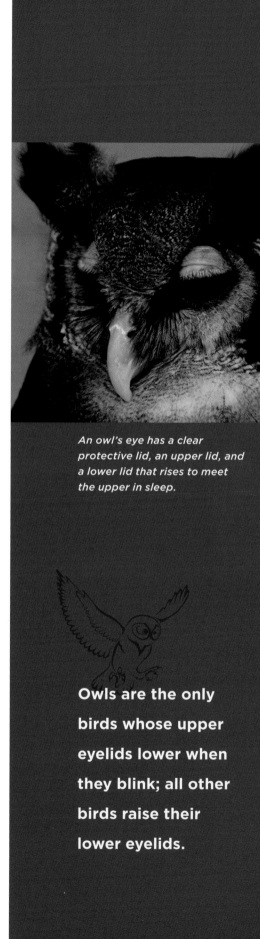

An owl's eye has a clear protective lid, an upper lid, and a lower lid that rises to meet the upper in sleep.

Owls are the only birds whose upper eyelids lower when they blink; all other birds raise their lower eyelids.

ANIMAL TALE: THE OWL'S SPOTS

Owls are considered sacred, or holy, creatures in many American Indian and Canadian First Nations cultures, and the beautiful feathers of these symbols of wisdom are typically reserved for the most important rituals. The Cherokee story of the owl and the young woman reveals why many owl species have spotted plumage.

Long ago, Owl hid in the forest because he believed his eyes were too big, his face was too flat, and his feathers were too plain. He felt ugly and believed that no one would ever love him. But a beautiful young woman befriended him, and because he spoke such words of wisdom and sang such soothing songs to her, she soon fell in love with Owl. The time came for Owl to ask the young woman's parents for her hand in marriage, so he went to her home to meet them. Because Owl felt ugly, he did not want the young woman's parents to see him, so when he arrived at the young woman's home in the evening, he hid in the shadowed corner of the room just outside the reach of the firelight.

Owl was wise and had great knowledge of many things. As he talked with the young woman's parents, they asked many questions and listened intently to Owl's wisdom. After Owl left, the young woman's parents told her that they believed Owl would be a good husband for her, but they were concerned by the fact that Owl had never stepped out of the shadows. They thought that perhaps Owl had something to hide. As the young woman and her parents continued to talk about Owl, the young woman's two mischievous brothers listened from the next room. They also wondered why Owl had hidden in the shadows and hatched a plan to reveal Owl on his next visit.

In the morning, the brothers went to the forest to gather firewood. They gathered up armloads of wood and returned home, which their mother thought was strange because the two boys were usually very lazy. Later that night, Owl returned to the young woman's home to visit with her family. The two brothers threw several pieces of wood on the fire—heavy oak logs that burned bright—but Owl remained hidden in the shadows just out of reach of the firelight.

Then the brothers threw sumac logs on the fire. They knew that sumac wood spits, pops, and throws sparks when burned. As the fire raged, the shadows in the room began to fade until Owl was nearly visible. The young woman's parents were shocked by Owl's ugly face and stepped away from him. Suddenly, sparks began to fly across the room, and Owl, in an effort to protect the young woman from the fire, hugged her close, wrapped his wings around her, and turned his back to the fire. The sparks landed on Owl's back and burned black spots on his coat of feathers.

The young woman's parents were very angry with the two brothers, but the incident proved to them that Owl truly loved their daughter. Despite Owl's big eyes and flat face, which the parents agreed were not very attractive, the parents blessed their daughter's marriage to Owl, whose coat is still speckled with the dark burns from the sumac logs.

GLOSSARY

Aborigines – the people who inhabited Australia before the arrival of European settlers

adapted – changed to improve its chances of survival in its environment

camouflage – the ability to hide, due to coloring or markings that blend in with a given environment

cultures – particular groups in a society that share behaviors and characteristics that are accepted as normal by that group

deforestation – the clearing away of trees from a forest

down – small feathers whose barbs do not interlock to form a flat surface, thus giving a fluffy appearance

egg tooth – a hard, toothlike tip of a young bird's beak or a young reptile's mouth, used only for breaking through its egg

encroachment – movement into an area already occupied

evolved – gradually developed into a new form

extinction – the act or process of becoming extinct; coming to an end or dying out

food chain – a system in nature in which living things are dependent on each other for food

Global Positioning System – a system of satellites, computers, and other electronic devices that work together to determine the location of objects or living things that carry a trackable device

incubate – to provide heat that promotes development or growth of a living thing

indigenous – originating in a particular region or country

migrate – to undertake a regular, seasonal journey from one place to another and then back again

mortality rate – the number of deaths in a certain area or period

mythology – a collection of myths, or popular, traditional beliefs or stories that explain how something came to be or that are associated with a person or object

nebula – a bright area in outer space that is made of a cloud of gas and dust

plumage – the entire feathery covering of a bird

regurgitated – having thrown up partially digested food

satellite – a mechanical device launched into space; it may be designed to travel around Earth or toward other planets or the sun

SELECTED BIBLIOGRAPHY

Burns, Jim. *Owls of North America: Journey Through a Shadowed World*. Minocqua, Wisc.: Willow Creek Books, 2004.

Duncan, James R. *Owls of the World: Their Lives, Behavior, and Survival*. Buffalo: Firefly Books, 2003.

Lynch, Wayne. *Owls of the United States and Canada: A Complete Guide to Their Biology and Behavior*. Baltimore: Johns Hopkins University Press, 2007.

The Owl Foundation. "Homepage." http://www.theowlfoundation.ca.

The Owl Pages. "Owl News Articles Index." http://www.owlpages.com/news.php.

Scholz, Floyd. *Owls*. Mechanicsburg, Penn.: Stackpole Books, 2001.

Having adapted to share the world with humans, owls are found in virtually every habitat on Earth.

INDEX